Louis Weber, CEO
Publications International, Ltd.
7373 North Cicero Avenue
Lincolnwood, Illinois 60712

Permission is never granted for commercial purposes.

ISBN-13: 978-1-4127-1323-8
ISBN-10: 1-4127-1323-4

Manufactured in China.

8 7 6 5 4 3 2 1

If Cats Could Talk

Written by Michael P. Fertig

Publications International, Ltd.

But if you have me declawed,
I won't be able to do *this* anymore!

Don't try to play cute with me, mister.

I saw you out with the dog.

Just looking at me made you yawn, didn't it?

This may be the longest nap I've ever taken.

If you really want something,
you just have to go in and get it yourself.

When the mouse laughs at the cat,
there is a hole nearby.

–Nigerian Proverb

Trust me. It'll be worth the effort.

The only thing better than a good stretch?
A good stretch in your sleep.

I am constantly amazed by my friend's complete lack of inhibitions.

Ears. Scratch. Now.

There is no shame
in not knowing...

...the shame lies
in not finding out.

—RUSSIAN PROVERB

I'm going to close my eyes,
and when I open them
I hope there's a squeaky toy in front of me.

For your sake.

Psst. Mouse. C'mere.

I've got something to show ya.

Dog shmog.

Tell me he isn't still staring at me.

All dressed up with no place to go.

Mission: Window Shade Pull String.

Decision: Accepted.

Oh, deer!

Although I look
fat and slow,
no one dares disobey
my posted rules.

41

I won't roll in *that* again.

Jim's Fish Market?

Do you deliver?

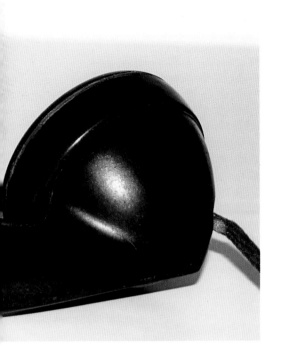

Find

your

place

in the

sun.

Then

take a

nap.

I trust my dinner is ready and waiting

for me in its usual spot.

Horrible conflict?

Or two unlikely friends

playing a game?

How many dogs does it take

to screw in a lightbulb?

All of 'em.

One to turn it, and the rest

to run around in circles and bark at it!

You are getting sleepy.

Your eyelids are getting heavy.

You want to give me a big can of tuna.

Canine Control 101.

After a long
day of lying
on the sofa,
I like to unwind by
rolling over
for a stretch
and a nap.

Who says bad things happen in threes?

Then you
shouldn't have
put the
dinner rolls
in *my*
basket.

Then is it *good* luck if I cross your path?

Even the dog knows *I'm* the boss.

Hard day. Hair ball. 'Nuf said.

One should be just as careful
in choosing one's pleasures
as in avoiding calamities.

–CHINESE PROVERB

Do *not*

sneak up

on me

like that.

It isn't the size of the human.

It's the size of the love in the human.

I wonder why
they called me Boots.

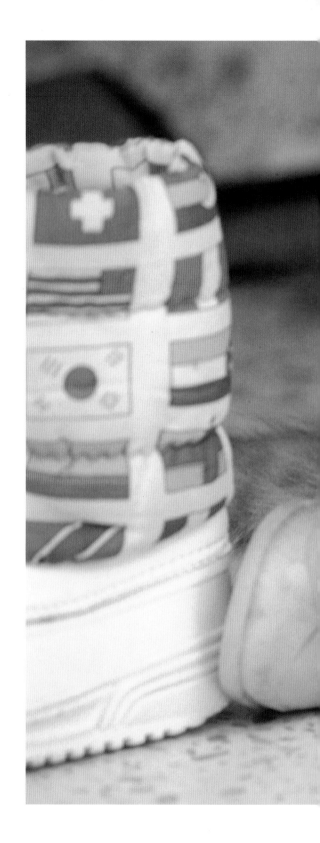

I want to turn over a new leaf....

or eat one,

and I just can't decide which.

People always
think I'm a
fat cat,
but believe me,
under all this fur
is the body of a
runway model.

Canary?

What canary?

How in the world am I supposed

to get back down?

During the summer
theater season
I learned to play dead.
Now it's just the
greatest trick to play
on people.

I put the *fur*
in *furniture*.

The things I'll put up with

to get some catnip!

Yes . . . you are correct.
I am a trick rider,
and all the horses fear me.

You want a piece of me?

Huh?

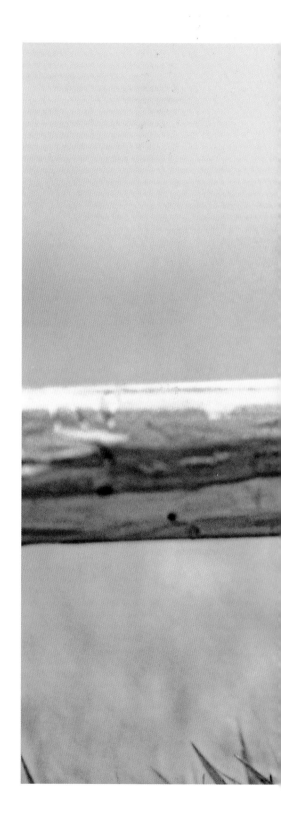